River Adventures

THE AMAZON RIVER

BY COLLEEN SEXTON

BLASTOFF! DISCOVERY

BELLWETHER MEDIA • MINNEAPOLIS, MN

Blastoff! Discovery launches a new mission: reading to learn. Filled with facts and features, each book offers you an exciting new world to explore!

This edition first published in 2025 by Bellwether Media, Inc.

Library of Congress Cataloging-in-Publication Data

Names: Sexton, Colleen A., 1967- author.
Title: The Amazon River / by Colleen Sexton.
Description: Minneapolis, MN : Bellwether Media, Inc., 2025. | Series: Blastoff! Discovery : River adventures | Includes bibliographical references and index. | Audience: Ages 7-13 | Audience: Grades 4-6 | Summary: "Engaging images accompany information about the Amazon River. The combination of high-interest subject matter and narrative text is intended for students in grades 3 through 8"– Provided by publisher.
Identifiers: LCCN 2024016550 (print) | LCCN 2024016551 (ebook) | ISBN 9798886879964 (library binding) | ISBN 9781644879283 (ebook)
Subjects: LCSH: Amazon River–Juvenile literature.
Classification: LCC F2546 .S5266 2025 (print) | LCC F2546 (ebook) | DDC 981/.1–dc23/eng/20240513
LC record available at https://lccn.loc.gov/2024016550
LC ebook record available at https://lccn.loc.gov/2024016551

Editor: Rachael Barnes Designer: Brittany McIntosh

Printed in the United States of America, North Mankato, MN.

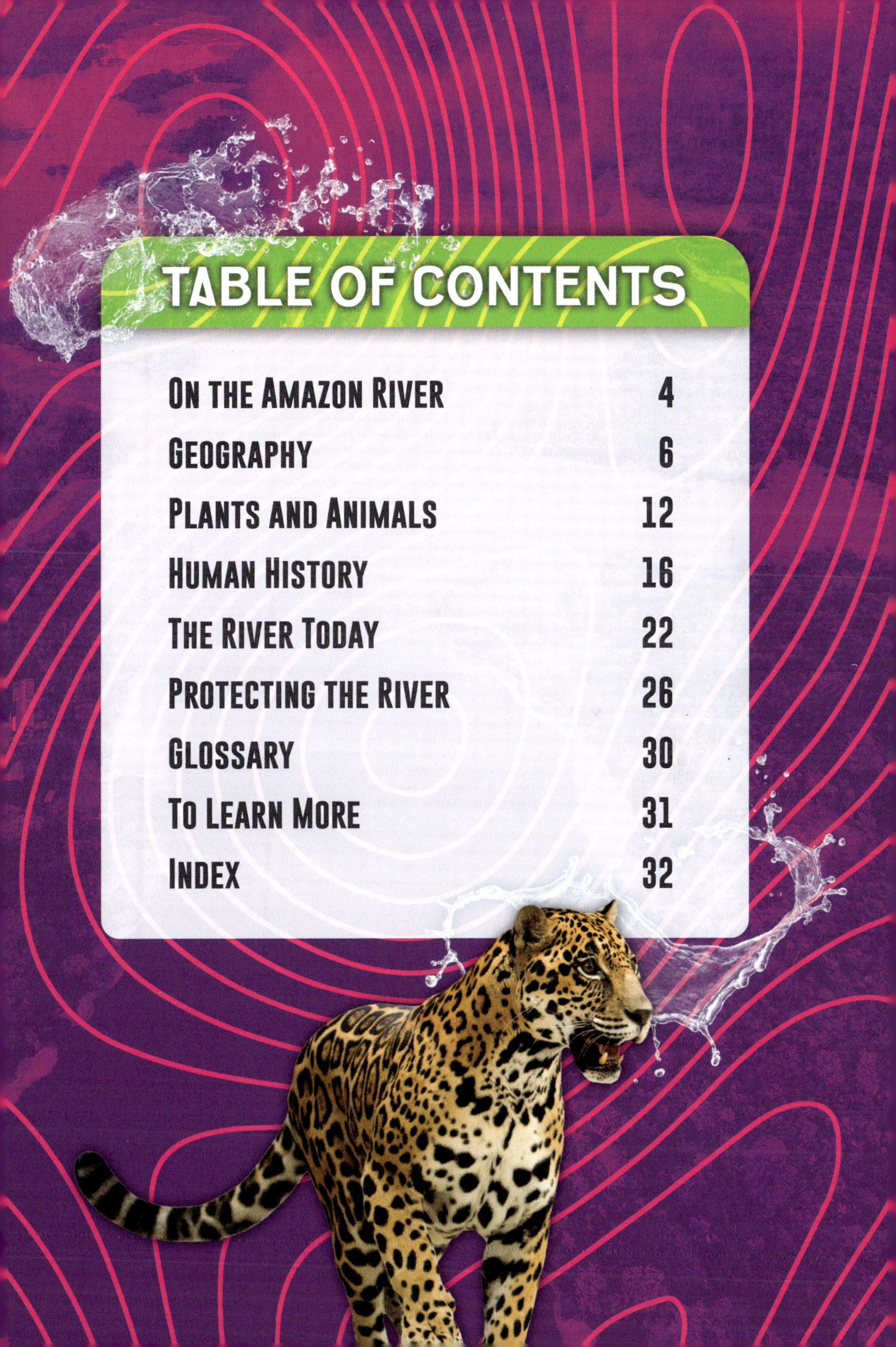

TABLE OF CONTENTS

ON THE AMAZON RIVER

A riverboat leaves Manaus, Brazil, on a four-day tour of the Amazon River. The day is sunny and hot. The cloudy brown water is calm. Trees in every shade of green line the riverbanks. Passengers look up at huge trees that reach toward the sky. They are in the Amazon Rain Forest.

MANAUS

Cargo ships enter the Amazon River from the Atlantic Ocean. They travel about 1,000 miles (1,609 kilometers) inland to dock in Manaus.

MANAUS, BRAZIL

The calls and chirps of animals fill the air. Passengers spot colorful birds and busy monkeys. Sometimes they pass villages with houses built on **stilts**. Boats of all sizes travel up and down the river. The passengers wave. Their Amazon River adventure is just beginning!

GEOGRAPHY

The Amazon is often called the "River Sea." It carries more water than any other river. It crosses South America for at least 4,000 miles (6,437 kilometers). Some believe the Amazon is the world's longest river. But most think it is slightly shorter than the Nile River.

The Amazon River's **source** is in Peru. It begins high in the Andes Mountains. The river flows northward down the mountains. It then flows east to the Peruvian port city of Iquitos. The Amazon crosses Brazil and flows past Manaus. It continues to Marajó Island before emptying into the Atlantic Ocean.

BIG ISLANDS

Near the Atlantic Ocean, the Amazon River splits into several waterways. This creates huge river islands. The largest is Marajó Island. It is about the size of Switzerland!

TIDAL WAVE

The high ocean tide at the Amazon River's mouth creates a huge wave. It is called a tidal bore. It rises up to 12 feet (3.7 meters) tall. Surfers often ride the wave as it rushes up the river!

ANDES MOUNTAINS

The Amazon River once flowed west. Over time, **tectonic plates** crashed together to form the Andes Mountains. They blocked the river's route. The water became a huge lake. About 10 million years ago, the water started to drain downhill. **Erosion** shaped a path for a new river to flow east into the Atlantic Ocean.

Today, the Amazon River is usually about 6 miles (10 kilometers) wide. During rainy months, the river can swell to over 6 times this width. Its average depth is 40 feet (12 meters). But some parts reach up to 300 feet (91 meters) deep!

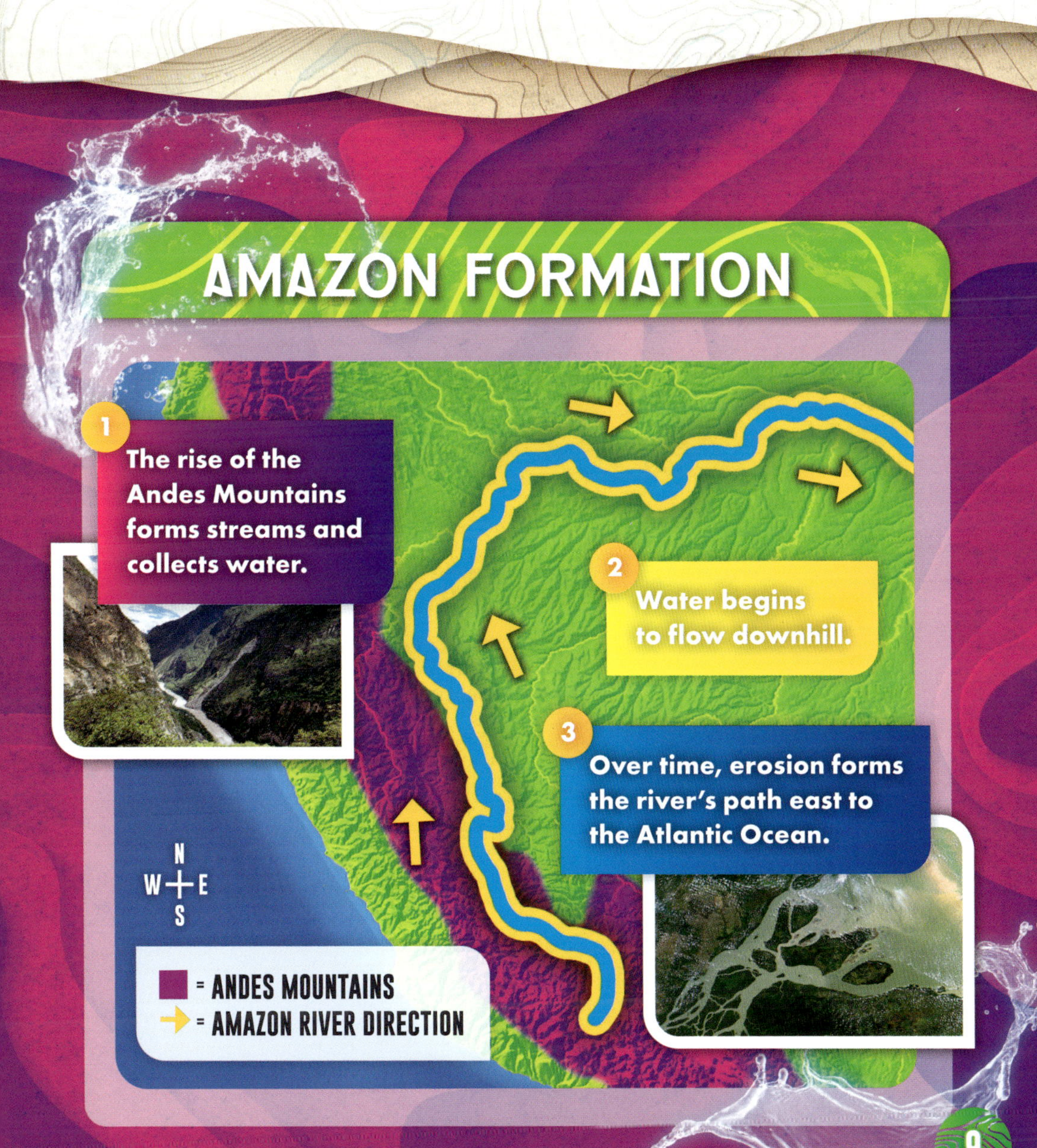

The Amazon River system is the world's largest river system. It has around 1,100 **tributaries**. The tributaries reach the Amazon from Brazil and seven nearby countries. The longest are over 1,000 miles (1,609 kilometers) long. They include the Madeira, Purus, Negro, and Japurá Rivers.

AMAZON RIVER

NEGRO RIVER

THE MEETING OF THE WATERS

The Negro River is often called *Rio Negro*. It is Spanish for "Black River." When it meets the Amazon River, the waters are two different colors until they mix!

The Amazon River system lies in the Amazon **Basin**. The region's rainfall collects in the rivers. Sometimes it combines with melting snow from the Andes Mountains. The water can rise by as much as 50 feet (15 meters). It spills over the riverbanks and floods parts of the basin.

PLANTS AND ANIMALS

The Amazon River supports one of the most **biodiverse** places on Earth. Manatees and pink river dolphins swim in deep waters. Near the shore, caimans and giant otters eat fish. Green anacondas slide along riverbanks hunting prey. Capybaras dive in the water to escape. The sweet scent of giant water lilies attracts scarab beetles.

In the Amazon Rain Forest, giant butterflies flutter between flowers. Red deer chomp on fallen fruit. Giant anteaters use their sticky tongues to eat termites. At night, vampire bats take flight to hunt. Jaguars, ocelots, and pumas prowl the forest floor.

SPECTACLED CAIMAN

GREEN ANACONDA

GIANT ANTEATER

CAPYBARA

VAMPIRE BAT

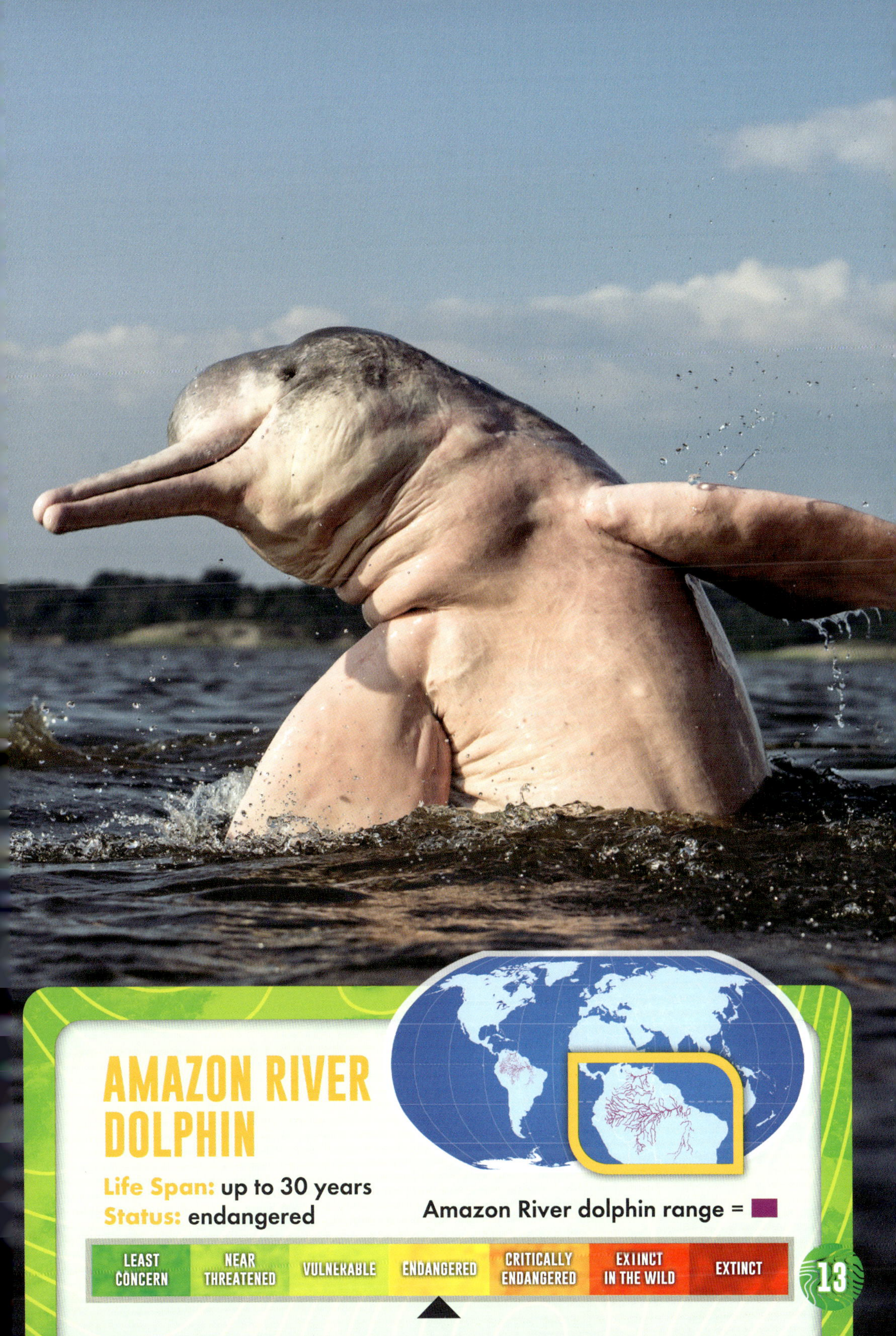
AMAZON RIVER DOLPHIN
Life Span: up to 30 years
Status: endangered
Amazon River dolphin range =
LEAST CONCERN
NEAR THREATENED
VULNERABLE
ENDANGERED
CRITICALLY ENDANGERED
EXTINCT IN THE WILD
EXTINCT

The Amazon River regularly floods large parts of the surrounding forests. Rich soil spreads with the water. Brazil nut, mahogany, rubber, and kapok trees grow tall. Thick liana vines wind around tree trunks. Monkeys leap from branch to branch. They pick fruit from palms. Branches also support spectacled bears and slow-moving sloths. Tree frogs leap into bromeliad plants.

THE TALLEST OF ALL

The tallest tree in the Amazon Rain Forest is an angelim vermelho. It grows in northern Brazil. It is 290 feet (88 meters) tall!

LIANA VINE

High among the trees, bees buzz around orchids while hummingbirds drink nectar from heliconia flowers. Brightly colored parrots, toucans, and parakeets fly in the treetops. Harpy eagles soar high overhead.

HUMAN HISTORY

The first humans arrived in the Amazon Basin at least 12,000 years ago. They traveled the rivers in rafts and dugout canoes. They hunted and caught fish. They collected fruits and plants from the rain forest. Over time, people built small villages and cleared land to grow crops.

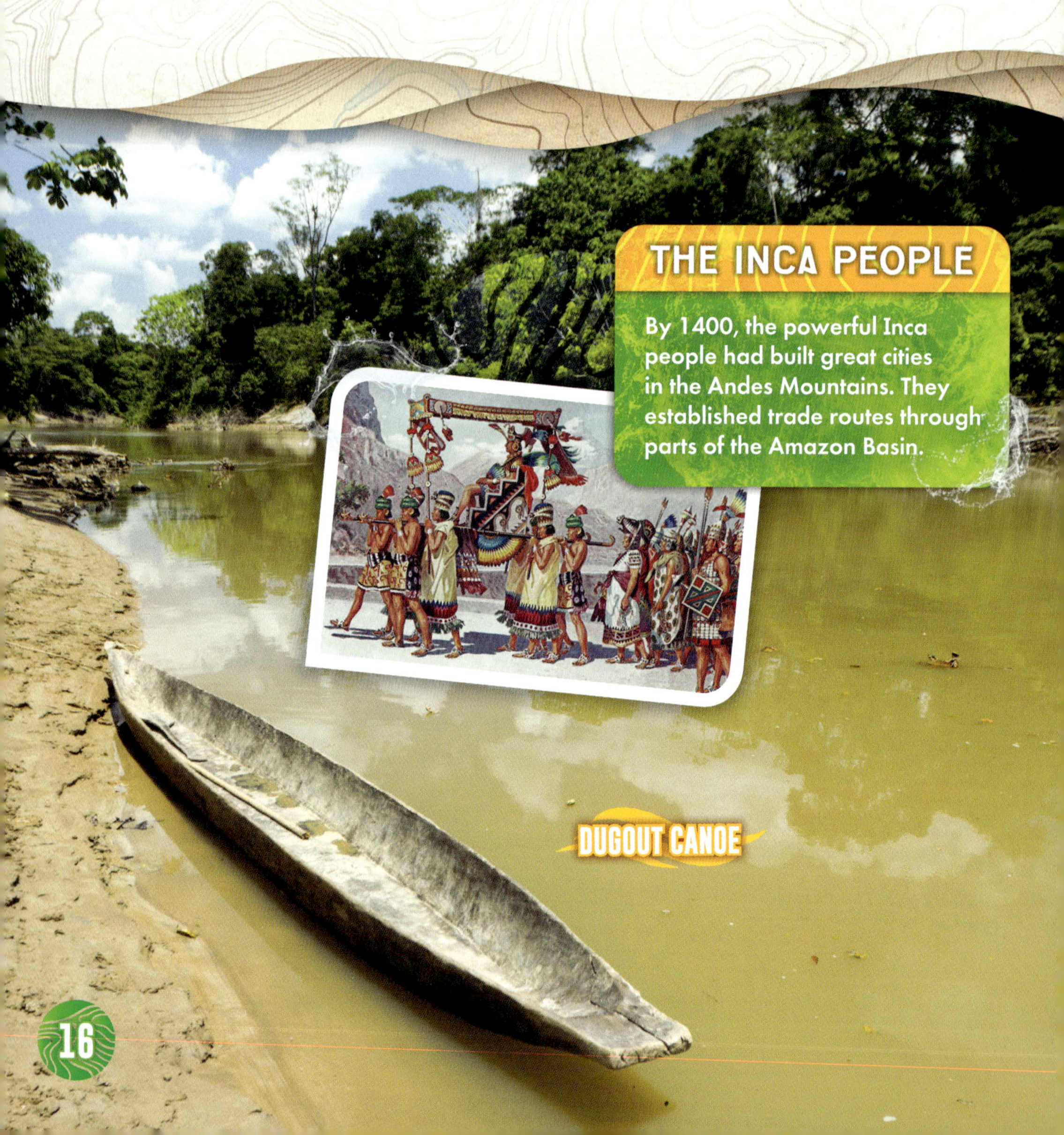

THE INCA PEOPLE

By 1400, the powerful Inca people had built great cities in the Andes Mountains. They established trade routes through parts of the Amazon Basin.

CULTURAL CONNECTION

EL DORADO

WHAT IS IT?

A city said to have great stores of gold

WHERE IS IT?

Thought by Europeans to be in the Amazon region but never found

MEANING TODAY

Any place with wealth and opportunities

By the late 1400s, Spain and Portugal wanted control of the Americas. They agreed Spain would control the western Americas. Portugal would control the east. In 1500, Spanish explorers searching for treasure became the first Europeans to reach the Amazon region. They traveled a short distance up the Amazon River and traded with **Indigenous** peoples.

Between 1541 and 1542, Spanish explorer Francisco de Orellana became the first European to travel the length of the Amazon River. He also gave the river its name. Later, Portuguese explorer Pedro Teixeira led a two-way **expedition** on the Amazon. His group traveled upstream from the **mouth** in 1637 and returned in 1639.

Millions of Indigenous peoples lived in the region when Europeans first arrived. However, Europeans brought deadly diseases. They also began stealing lands and **enslaving** many people. This continued for centuries. Thousands of Indigenous peoples died.

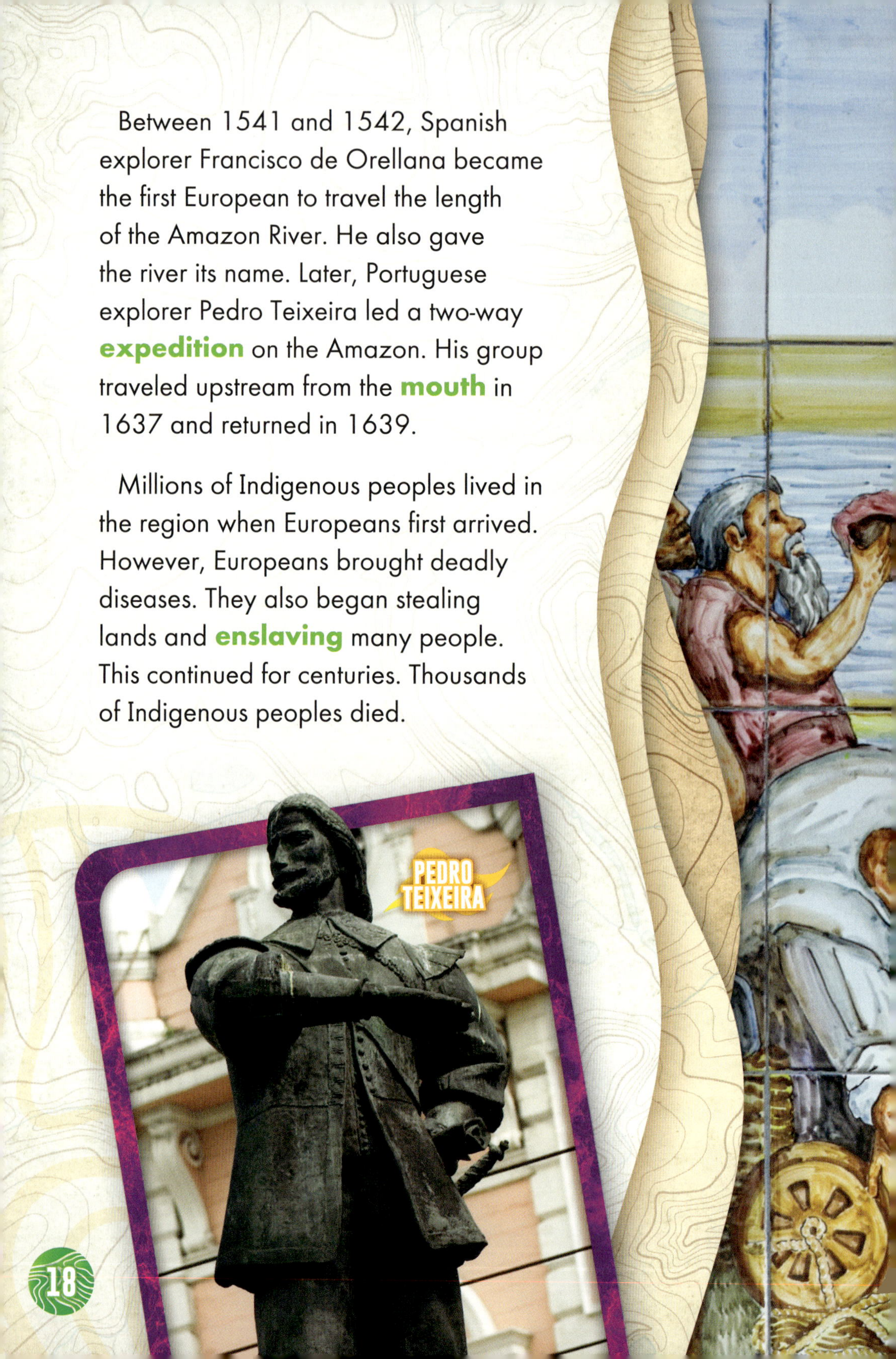

PEDRO TEIXEIRA

FRANCISCO
DE ORELLANA

THE RUBBER BOOM

The Amazon Basin became part of a "rubber boom" in the mid-1800s. Workers tapped rubber trees and transported their harvest down the Amazon River to ocean ports. People used rubber to make tires, hoses, and other goods.

MISSIONARY CHURCH

Missionaries from Spain and Portugal also came to the Amazon region. They wanted Indigenous peoples to become Christians. The missionaries made maps of the area as they traveled. They also took notes about the wildlife they saw.

These records helped scientists study the Amazon Basin. Scientists Alexander von Humboldt and Aimé Bonpland arrived in 1799. They explored on foot and by canoe. Indigenous guides taught them about thousands of plants and animals. Their findings drew attention from people around the world. Many scientists traveled to the region in the following centuries.

AMAZON RIVER TIMELINE

1400s
About 8 to 10 million Indigenous people live in the Amazon Basin

1541
Spanish explorer Francisco de Orellana begins his journey down the Amazon River from the Andes Mountains to the Atlantic Ocean

1637
Portuguese explorer Pedro Teixeira leads an expedition upstream and returns in 1639

1799
Scientists Alexander von Humboldt and Aimé Bonpland arrive to study the Amazon Basin's wildlife and resources

2002
The Amazon Region Protected Areas program is formed to protect large areas of the Amazon

THE RIVER TODAY

SEAPLANE

CROSSING THE AMAZON

The Amazon River does not have any bridges. Most people must cross it by boat.

The population continues to grow along the Amazon River. Cities and towns are growing to keep up. Many Indigenous peoples have moved from deep in the rain forest to villages along riverbanks. The region depends on the Amazon River for food. The fishing **industry** provides fish to local markets. Many Indigenous tribes bring in a daily catch.

The Amazon River is a busy transportation route. It connects cities, towns, and Indigenous villages. Locals use canoes and small motorboats for short trips. Slow boats carry passengers and supplies long distances. Seaplanes use the Amazon River as a runway.

TRANSPORTATION PROFILE

SLOW BOATS OR *LANCHAS*

WHAT IS IT?

A type of riverboat with two or more levels that provides a low-cost way for passengers to travel long distances

PURPOSE

Carries passengers and cargo such as food, fuel, and other supplies

FUN FACT

Passengers often hang hammocks inside lanchas for sleeping on longer trips

BOAT MOVING GOODS NEAR MANAUS, BRAZIL

The Amazon River is a major trade route. It is wide enough for oceangoing ships to travel from the Atlantic Ocean to Iquitos, Peru. This route is about 2,300 miles (3,701 kilometers) long. Many ships and smaller boats bring clothes, oil, food, and other goods to the Amazon region. They often pick up tropical fruits and nuts, as well as lumber and rubber.

FLOATING HOSPITALS

Many small communities lie far away from a hospital. They depend on hospital ships that travel the Amazon River to provide medical care.

Ecotourism is a big business on the Amazon River. People visit from all around the world. Riverboats and cruise ships carry passengers. Guides tell visitors about the rain forest and the people, plants, and animals that live there.

PROTECTING THE RIVER

Pollution is a danger to the Amazon River. One cause is **deforestation** in the Amazon Rain Forest. People cut down trees to make room for farmland, ranches, and roads. Tree roots cannot hold soil in place. Wind and rain then carry soil into the river along with harmful chemicals. Millions of people could be left with unsafe drinking water.

Many people are working to stop these harmful practices. Some groups help farmers plant cacao and other tree crops that will keep the soil in place. Governments in the region have set aside large parts of the rain forest where people cannot clear trees.

POLLUTION

CACAO TREE

A SHRINKING RAIN FOREST

Pictures taken from space show how much the Amazon Rain Forest has shrunk. In the last 40 years, over 386,102 square miles (1,000,000 square kilometers) of the rain forest have been cut down.

DEFORESTATION IN BRAZIL

Climate change has led to **droughts** in the Amazon Basin. Less rainwater is flowing into the river system. There is less fresh water to drink and to grow food. The river can become too shallow for ships. The water temperature also rises, harming fish and other river life.

CATCHING THE SUN

People have started using electric boats powered by solar energy on the Amazon River. Solar energy comes from the sun and does not create harmful pollution.

The Amazon River carries the most fresh water of any river system in the world. It also supports the greatest variety of animals and plants on Earth. Governments and people around the world understand the river's importance. They are working to slow climate change and save the Amazon River.

GLOSSARY

basin—the area drained by a river

biodiverse—relating to the variety of life found in a certain place

climate change—a human-caused change in Earth's weather due to warming temperatures

deforestation—the act of cutting down a wide area of trees

droughts—long periods of dry weather

ecotourism—the business of people traveling to other places to learn about their natural environment

enslaving—considering people property and forcing them to work for no pay

erosion—the process through which rocks are worn away by wind, water, or ice

expedition—a journey with a purpose, such as to explore an area

Indigenous—related to a group of people that began in the area

industry—a group of businesses that provide a certain product

missionaries—people sent to a place to spread a religious faith

mouth—the place where a river empties into a larger body of water

source—the beginning of a river

stilts—poles used to support a structure above the ground or water level; stilts help protect houses from flooding.

tectonic plates—large pieces of the earth's crust

tributaries—rivers and streams that flow into a larger stream, river, or lake

TO LEARN MORE

AT THE LIBRARY

Francis, Sangma. *Amazon River.* Los Angeles, Calif.: Flying Eye Books, 2021.

Mehnert, Volker. *Great Rivers of the World.* New York, N.Y.: Prestel Publishing, 2021.

Rathburn, Betsy. *Exploring the Amazon.* Minneapolis, Minn.: Bellwether Media, 2023.

ON THE WEB

FACTSURFER

Factsurfer.com gives you a safe, fun way to find more information.

1. Go to www.factsurfer.com.

2. Enter "Amazon River" into the search box and click 🔍.

3. Select your book cover to see a list of related content.

INDEX

The images in this book are reproduced through the courtesy of: worldclassphoto, front cover, pp. 4-5; Anna Kaewkhammul, p. 3; ByDroneVideos, p. 5 (Manaus); John Warburton-Lee Photography/ Alamy, pp. 6-7; MBV1, p. 7 (Marajó Island); DanielPrudek/ iStock, p. 8; Eraldo Peres/ AP Images, p. 8 (tidal bore); DanielPrudek, p. 9 (left); Universal Images Group North America LLC/ Alamy, p. 9 (right); PARALAXIS, pp. 10 (top), 26-27; Arnika Ganten, p. 10 (bottom); Caio Pederneiras, p. 11; Giedriius, p. 12 (capybara); slowmotiongli, p. 12 (caiman); Emma Rietveld, p. 12 (anaconda); Elen Marlen, p. 12 (giant anteater); Michael Lynch, p. 12 (vampire bat); COULANGES, p. 13; Lukas Kovarik, p. 14 (sloth); PhotoSpirit/ Alamy, p. 14 (angelim vermelho); Dr Morley Read, pp. 14 (liana vines), 16; Jo Reason, p. 15; Herbert M. Herget/ Wikipedia, p. 16 (Inca people); duncan1890/ Getty Images, p. 17; Rolf Richardson/ Alamy, p. 18; WH_Pics, pp. 18-19; Barna Tanko, p. 20; phichet chaiyabin, p. 20 (rubber trees); Digital Image Library/ Alamy, p. 21 (Francisco de Orellana); Marcos Amend, p. 21 (Amazon region); Friedrich Georg Weitsch/ Wikipedia, p. 21 (Humboldt and Bonpland); Cavan Images/ Alamy, p. 22; MBV/ Alamy, p. 23; James Davis Photography, pp. 24-25; David Vilaplana/ Alamy, p. 25 (floating hospital); Frank Sanchez/ Alamy, p. 25 (ecotourism); juerginho, p. 26 (left); SL-Photography, p. 26 (right); Alexander Gerst/ Wikipedia, p. 27 (inset); Edmar Barros/ AP Images, p. 28; mariusz_prusaczyk/ iStockphoto, pp. 28-29; Photoongraphy, p. 31.